INSIDE IN THE INSIDE OUT
KOOKS

GUITAR
TAB
EDITION

D1152250

WISE PUBLICATIONS
PART OF THE MUSIC SALES GROUP
LONDON/NEW YORK/PARIS/SYDNEY/COPENHAGEN/BERLIN/MADRID/TOKYO

PUBLISHED BY
WISE PUBLICATIONS
14-15 BERNERS STREET, LONDON, W1T 3LJ, UK.

EXCLUSIVE DISTRIBUTORS:
MUSIC SALES LIMITED
DISTRIBUTION CENTRE, NEWMARKET ROAD,
BURY ST EDMUNDS, SUFFOLK, IP33 3YB, UK.

MUSIC SALES PTY LIMITED
120 ROTHSCHILD AVENUE, ROSEBERY,
NSW 2018, AUSTRALIA.

ORDER NO. AM986161
ISBN 1-84609-628-6
THIS BOOK © COPYRIGHT 2006 WISE PUBLICATIONS,
A DIVISION OF MUSIC SALES LIMITED.

EDITED BY DAVID WESTON.
MUSIC ARRANGED BY MATT COWE AND MARTIN SHELLARD.
MUSIC PROCESSED BY PAUL EWERS MUSIC DESIGN.

PRINTED IN THE EU.

WWW.MUSICSALES.COM

Seaside

Words & Music by
Luke Pritchard, Hugh Harris, Max Rafferty & Paul Garred

Eddie's Gun

Words & Music by
Luke Pritchard, Hugh Harris, Max Rafferty & Paul Garred

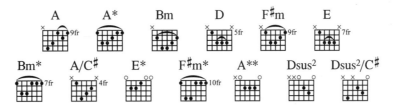

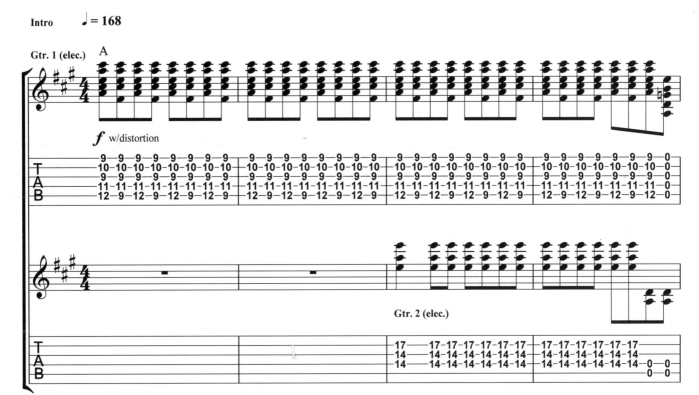

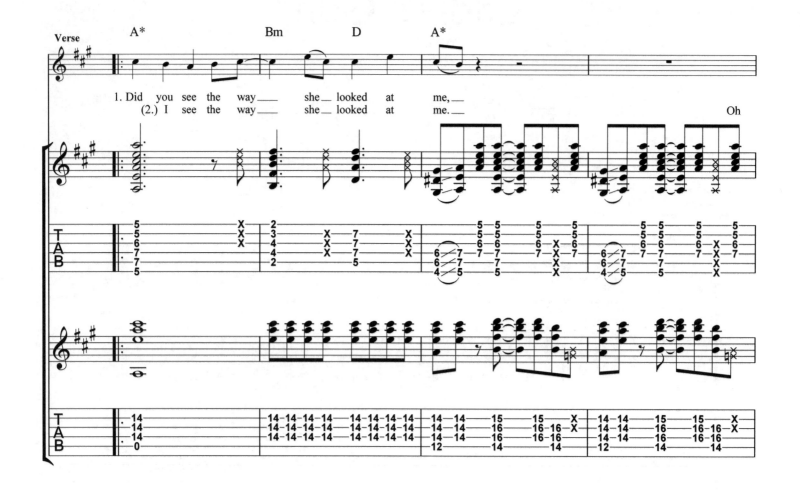

Verse

A*   **Bm**   **D**   **A***

1. Did you see the way____ she__ looked at me,____
(2.) I see the way____ she__ looked at me.____ Oh

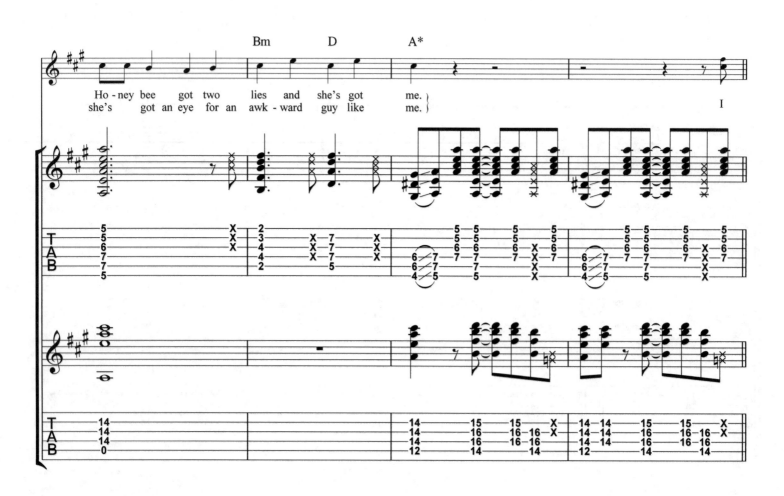

Bm   **D**   **A***

Ho - ney bee got two lies and she's got me.
she's got an eye for an awk - ward guy like me. } I

18

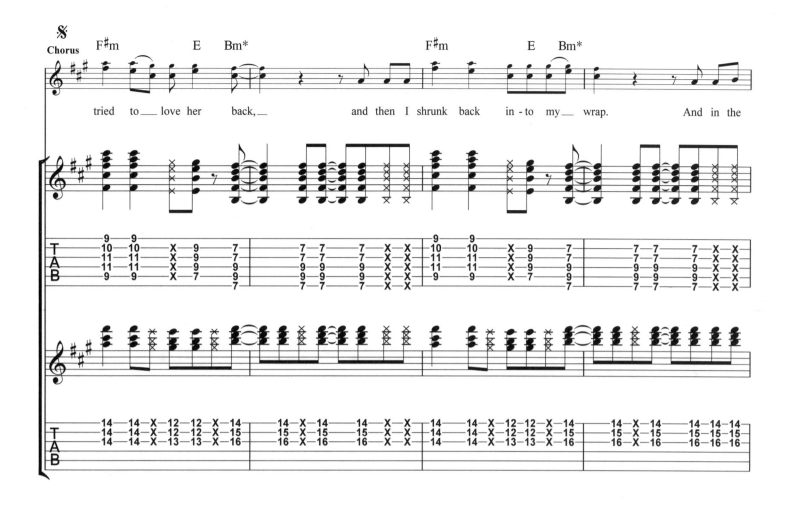

tried to___ love her back,___ and then I shrunk back in-to my___ wrap. And in the

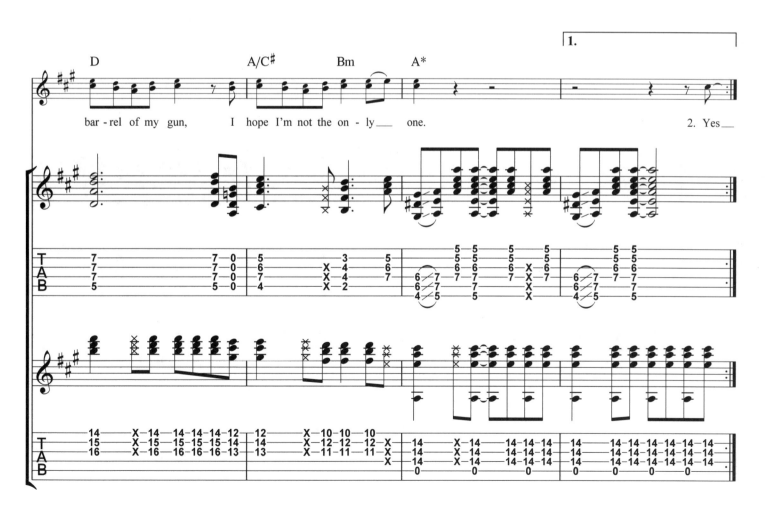

bar - rel of my gun, I hope I'm not the on - ly___ one. 2. Yes___

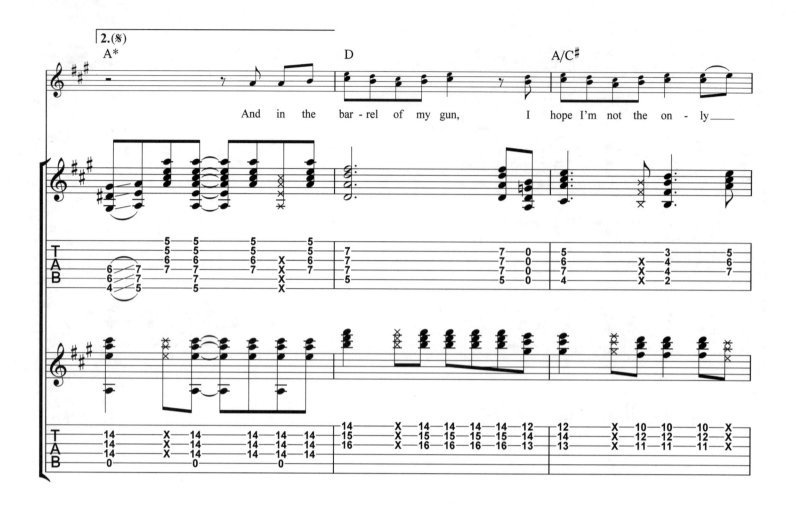

2.(𝄋)

And in the bar-rel of my gun, I hope I'm not the on-ly___

To Coda ⊕

one.

Yeah!

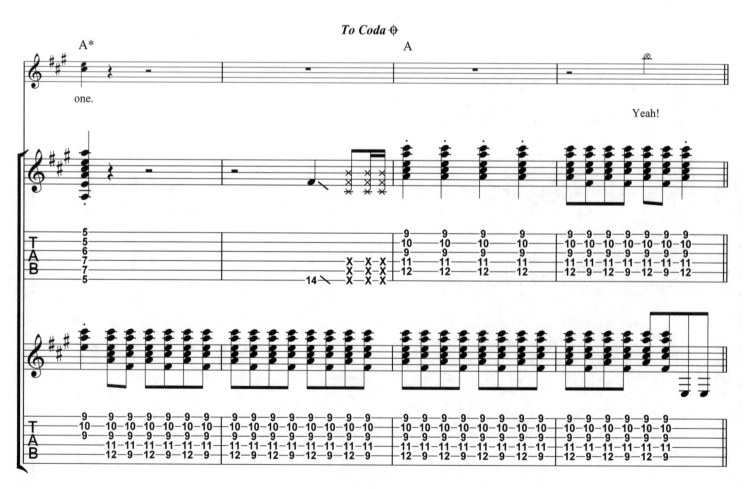

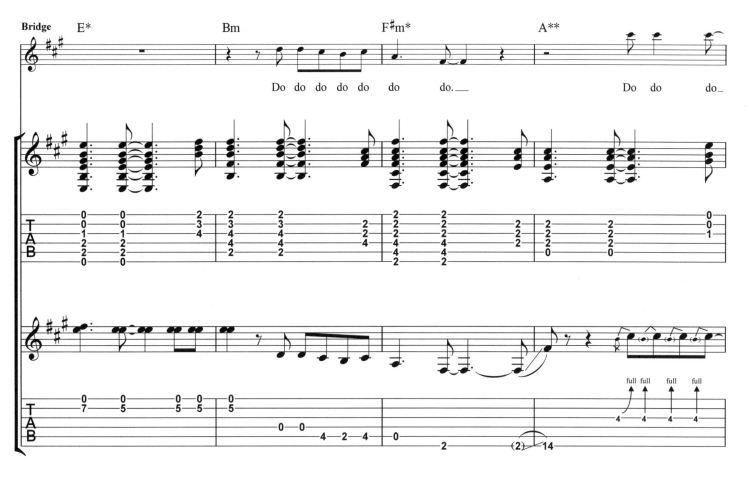

Bridge

Do do do do do do do. ___   Do do do ___

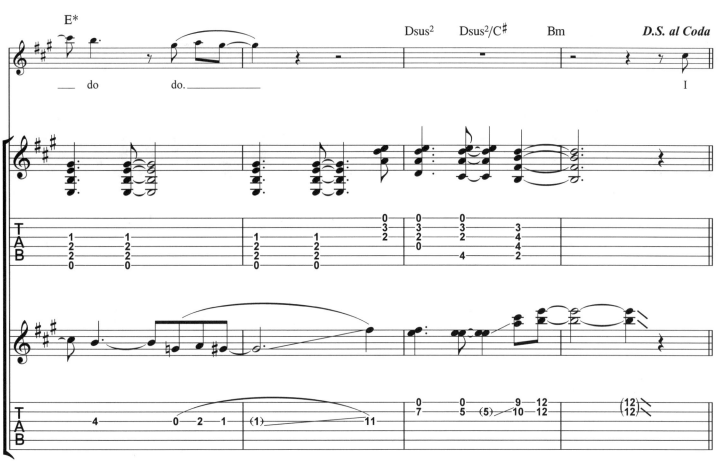

___ do   do. ___

D.S. al Coda

I

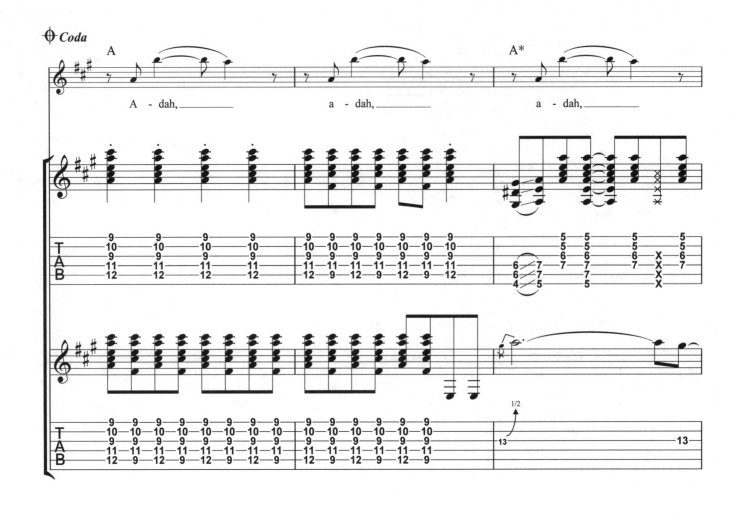

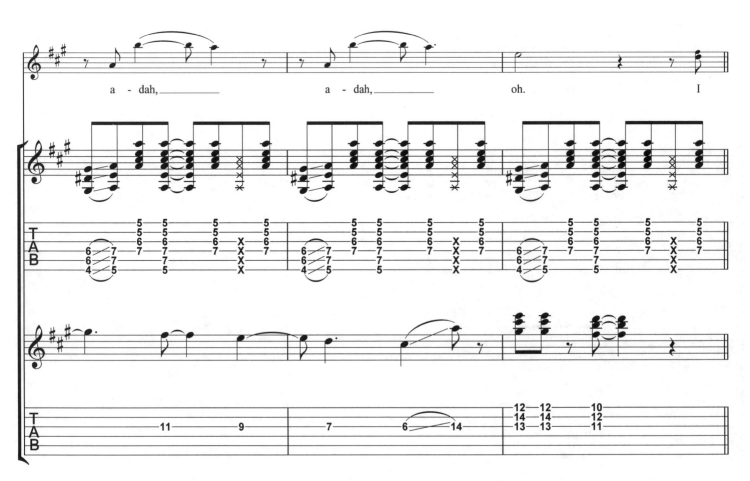

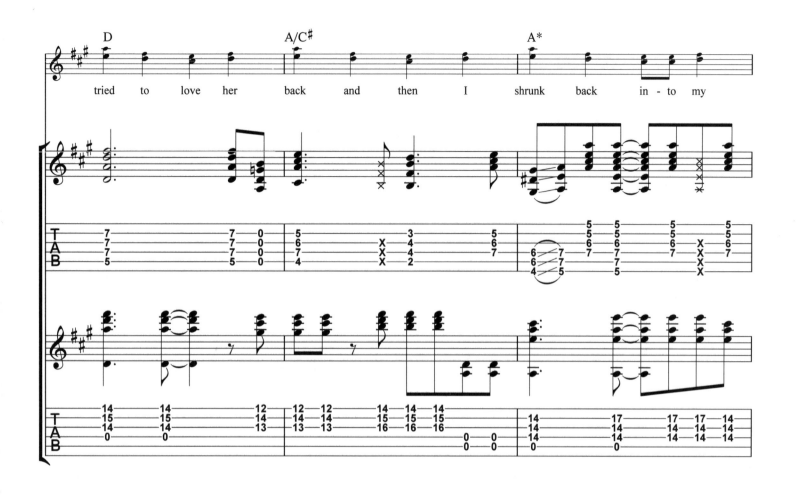

tried   to   love   her   back   and   then   I   shrunk   back   in - to   my

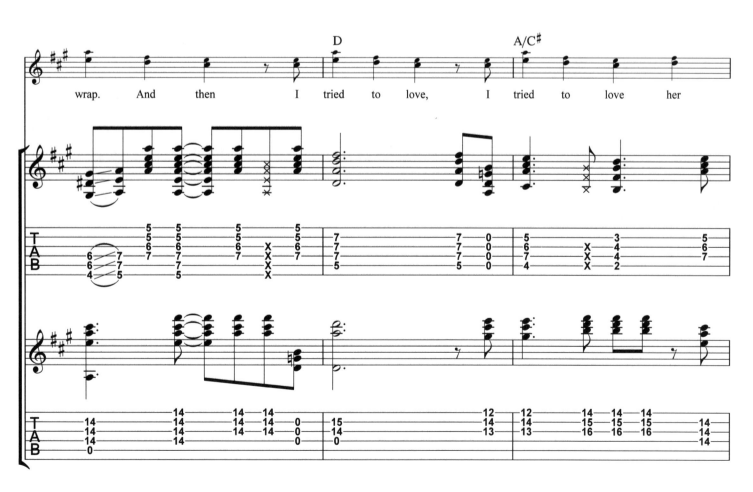

wrap.   And   then   I   tried   to   love,   I   tried   to   love   her

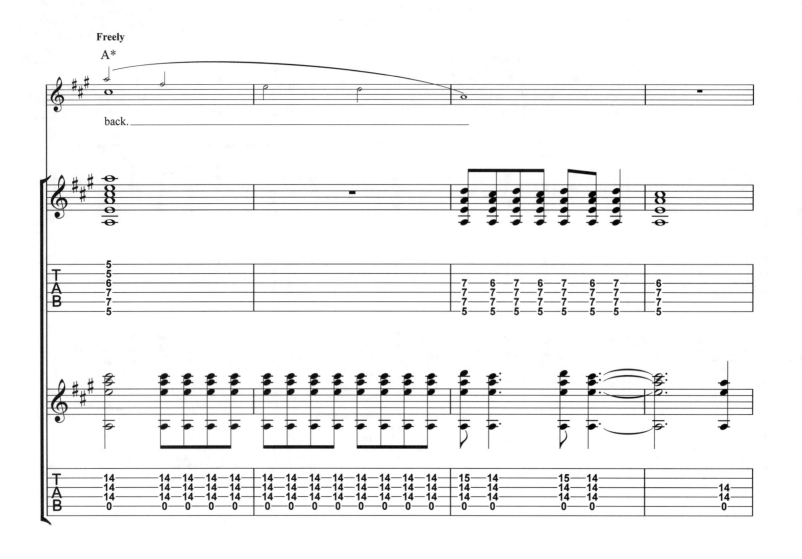

Ooh La

Words & Music by
Luke Pritchard, Hugh Harris, Max Rafferty & Paul Garred

You Don't Love Me

Words & Music by
Luke Pritchard, Hugh Harris, Max Rafferty & Paul Garred

29

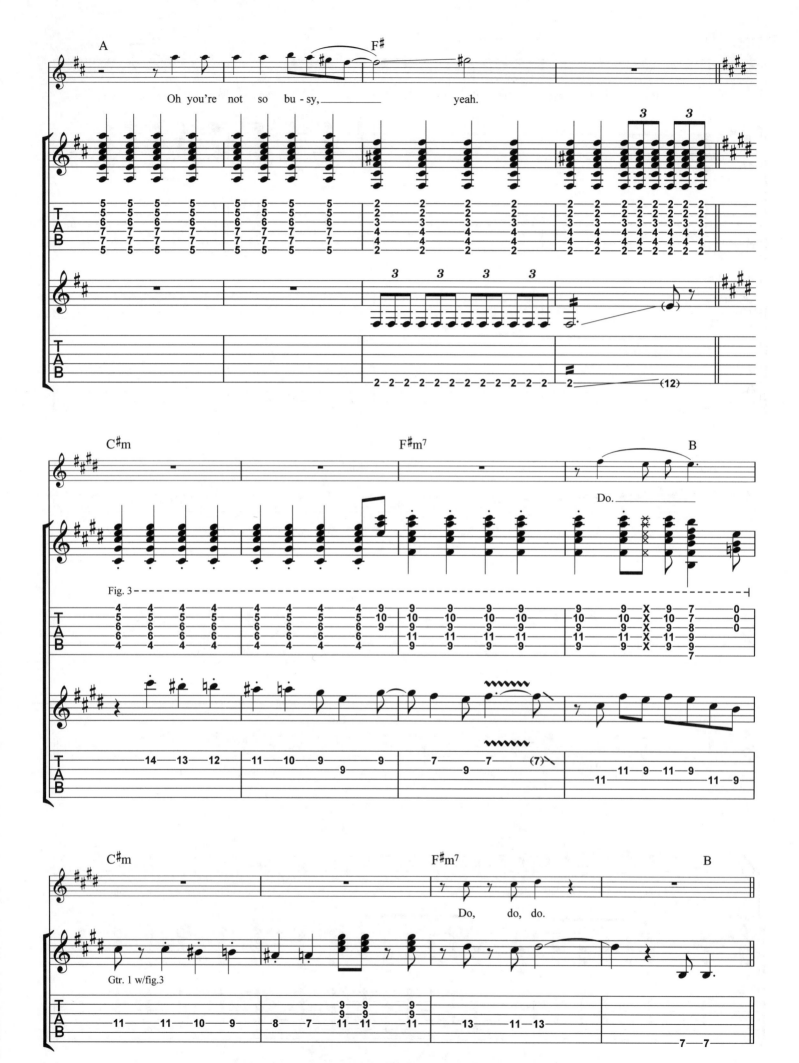

Verse C#m Gtr. 1 w/Fig. 3 *(x2)* F#m7 B

4. You don't love___ me you___ don't care,_____ wo - man.

C#m F#m7 B

You don't love___ me you___ don't care,_____ oh wo - man.

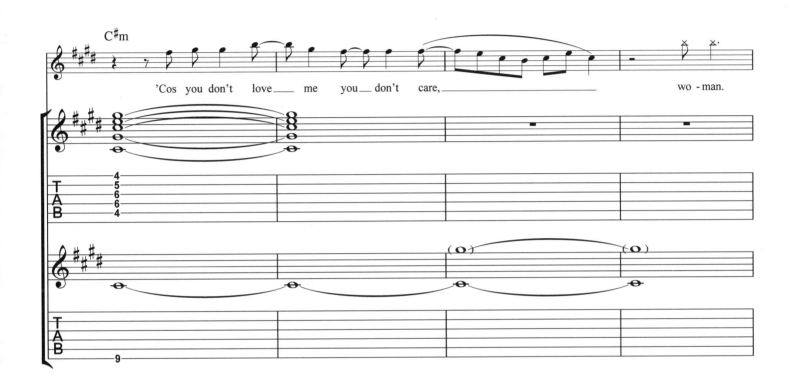

C#m

'Cos you don't love___ me you___ don't care,_____ wo - man.

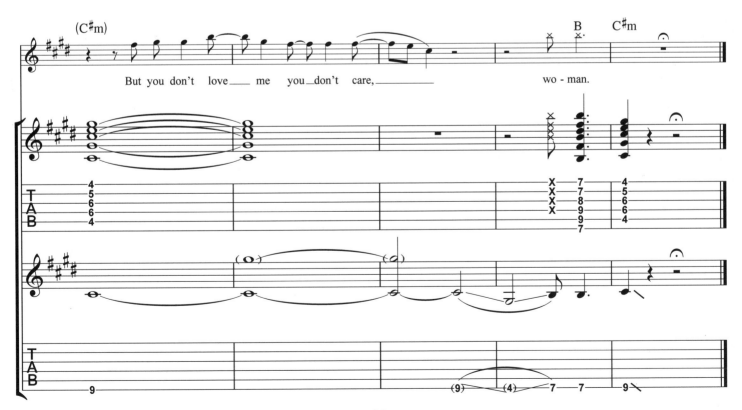

(C#m) B C#m

But you don't love___ me you___don't care,_____ wo - man.

She Moves In Her Own Way

Words & Music by
Luke Pritchard, Hugh Harris, Max Rafferty & Paul Garred

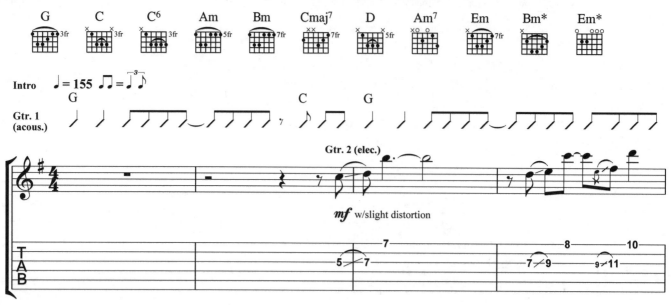

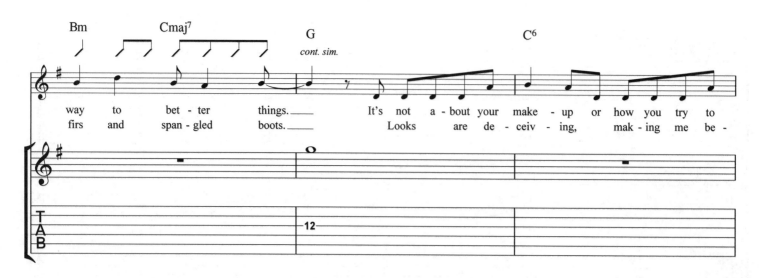

34

And kept them up___ in-stead of kick-ing us back___ down___ to the sub-urbs.

Solo

But uh oh,___ I love her be-cause___ she moves in her___ own way.

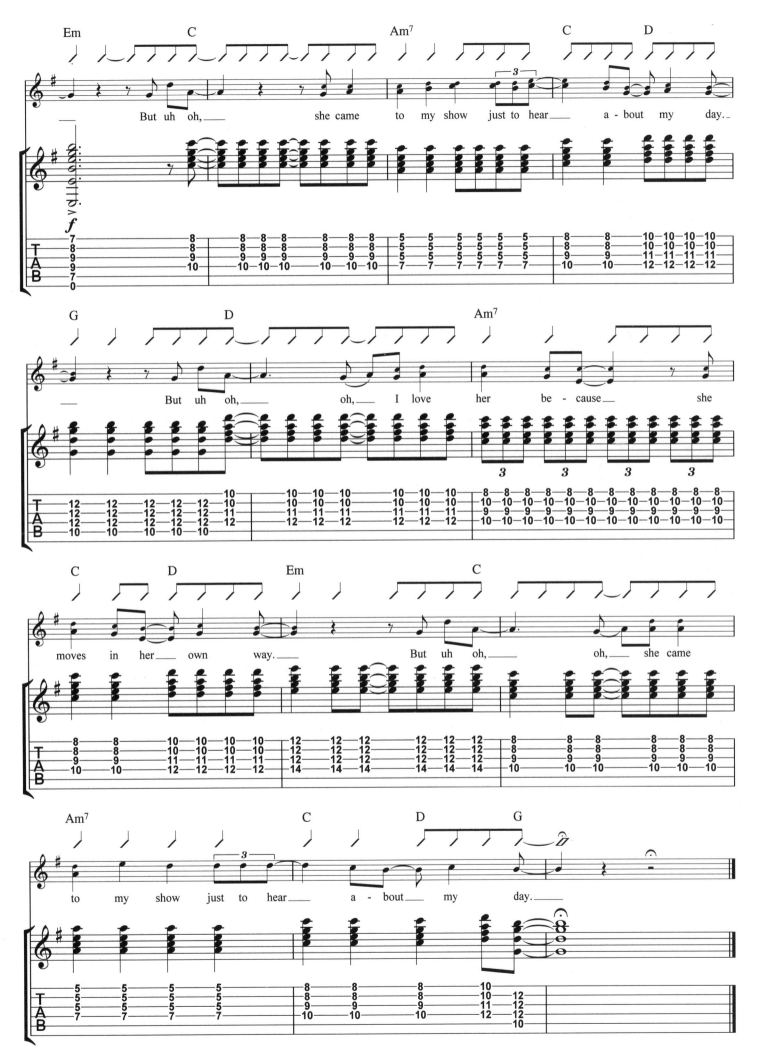

Matchbox

Words & Music by
Luke Pritchard, Hugh Harris, Max Rafferty & Paul Garred

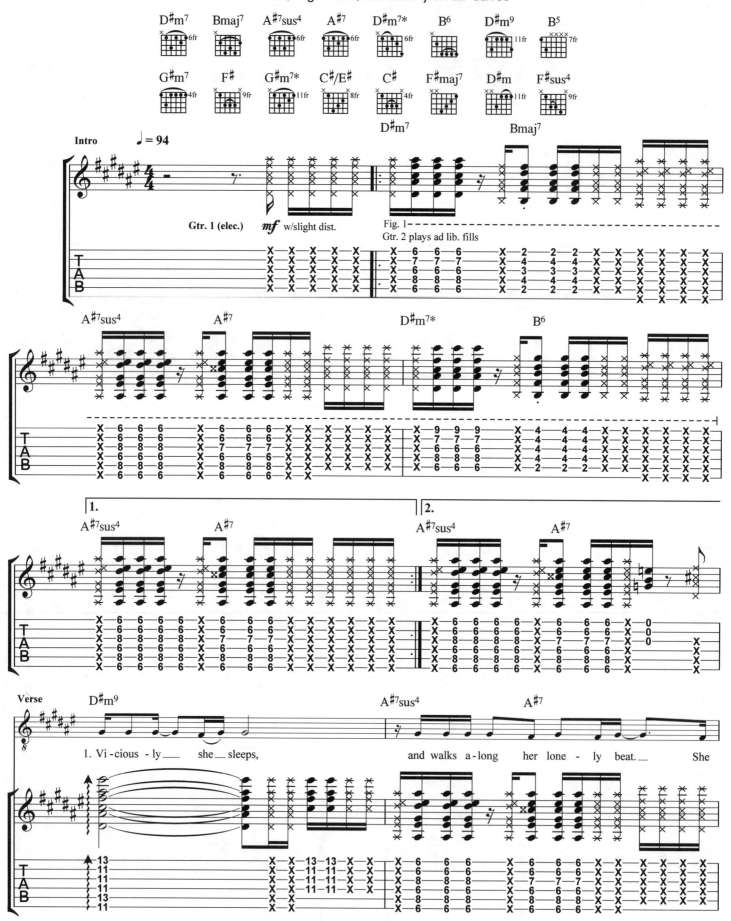

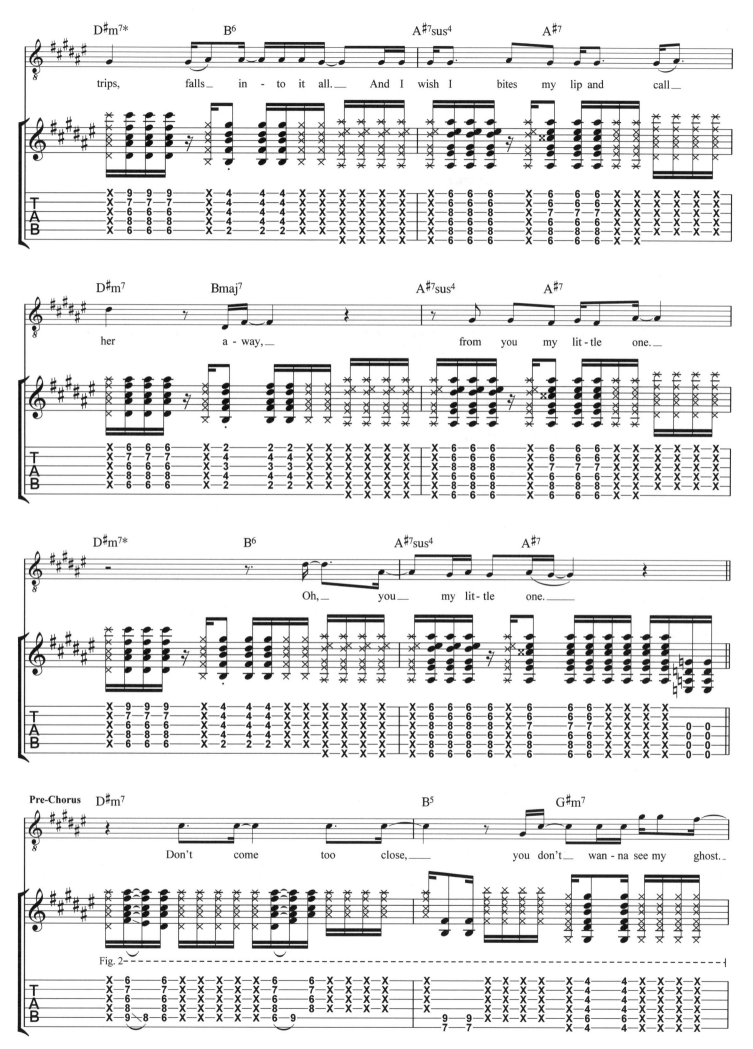

Gtr. 1w/Fig. 2

D#m7   B5   G#m7

_ Your turn_ but I'm_ be - trayed_ by you_ my sweet - heart.

D#m7   B5   G#m7

And don't you think_ that you went_ too far?_ And do you want_ to see my heart bleed?

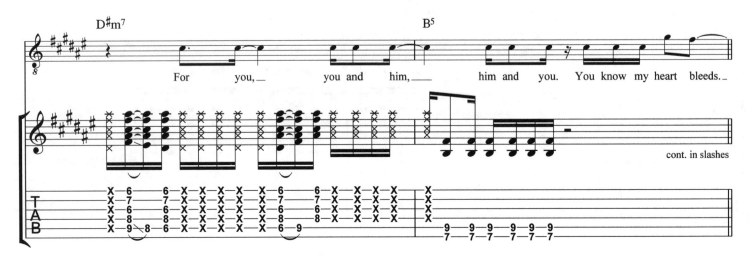

D#m7   B5

For you,_ you and him,_ him and you. You know my heart bleeds._

cont. in slashes

♩ = 188

§
Chorus
Gtrs.
1+2 (elec.)

D#m7   F#   G#m7*   F#   C#/E#
cont. sim.

_ And all of us,_ we're go - ing out to - night. We're gon - na walk all ov - er your

D#m7   F#   G#m7*   F#   C#/E#   D#m7

cars. The Kooks are out,_ in _ the street._ Oh,_ we're gon - na_ steal your skies._ All of us,_

F#   G#m7*   F#   C#/E#

_ we're go - ing out to - night. We're gon - na walk all ov - er your

To Coda ⊕

D#m7   F#   G#m7*   F#   C#/E#

cars. The Kooks are out,_ in _ the street._ Oh,_ they're gon - na_ steal your. 2. I'm

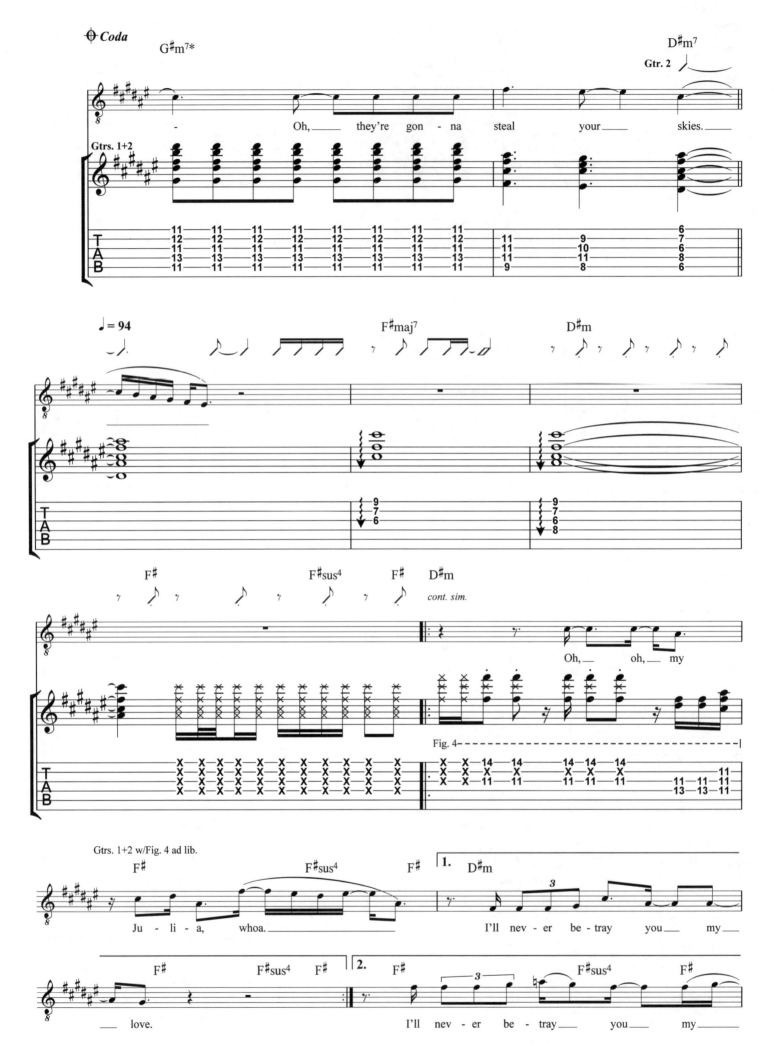

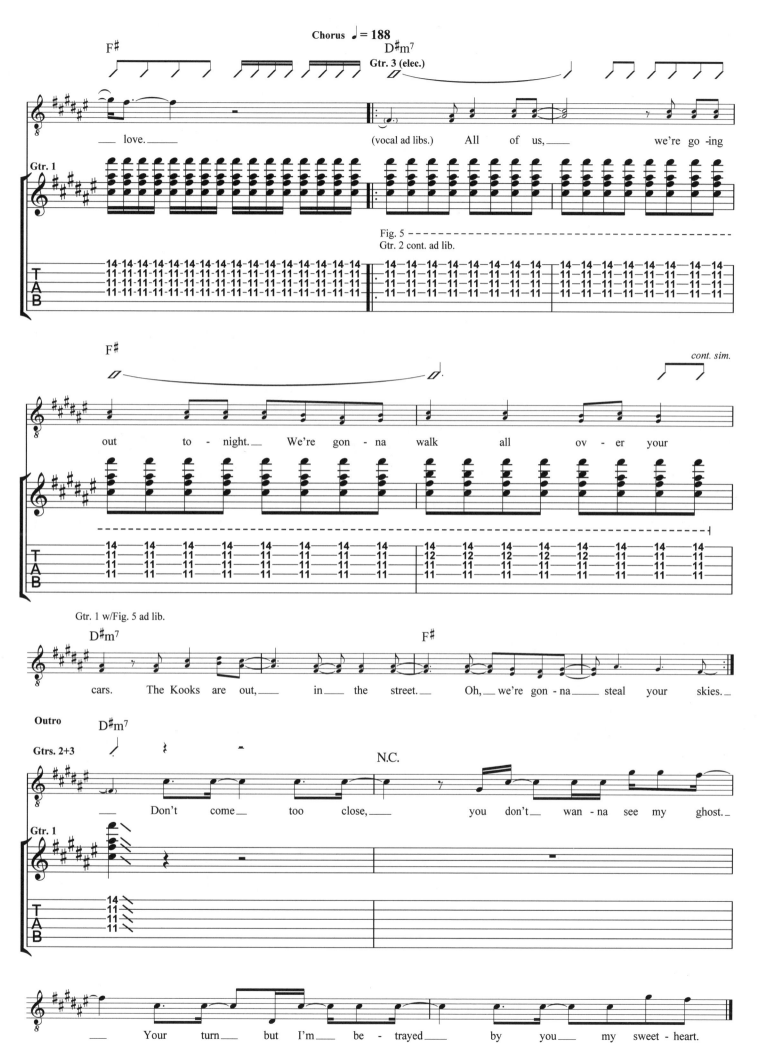

45

Naïve

Words & Music by
Luke Pritchard, Hugh Harris, Max Rafferty & Paul Garred

All Gtrs. Capo 4th fret

Gtr. 1 w/Fig.1

How could this be done by such a smiling sweet‑heart? Oh

and your sweet and pret‑ty face? In such an ug‑ly way,

for some‑thing so beau‑ti‑ful. Oh, that ev'‑ry‑time I look in‑side.

Chorus

Gtrs. 1+2 (elec.)

I know she knows that I'm not fond of ask‑ing. True or false it may be,

but she's still out to get me. And I know she knows that I'm not fond of ask‑ing.

Gtr. 1 (Gtr. 2 plays ad lib.)

True or false it may be, but she's still out to get me.

Gtr. 1 w/Fig.1
Gtr. 2 plays ad lib.

Verse

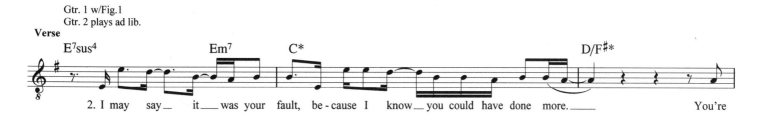

2. I may say it was your fault, be‑cause I know you could have done more. You're

47

49

I Want You

Words & Music by
Luke Pritchard, Hugh Harris, Max Rafferty & Paul Garred

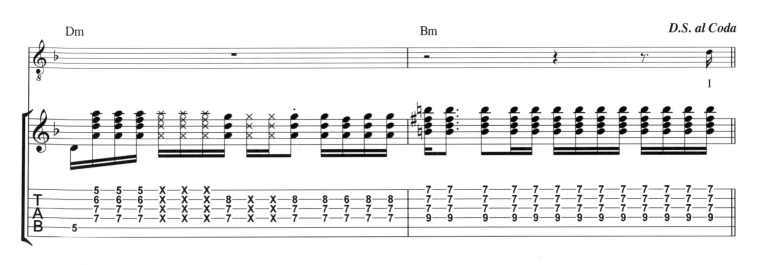

want your_____ love. But I can't let my - self love_____ you._

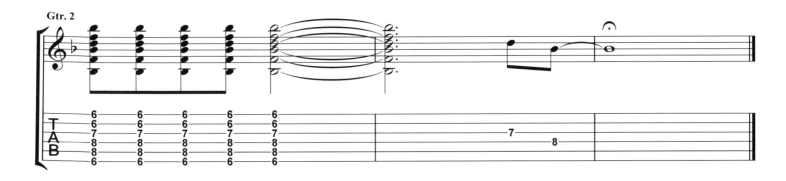

53

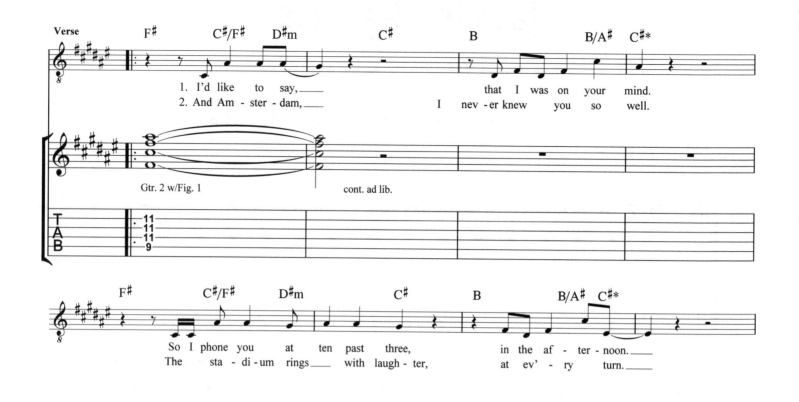

Verse

F♯ C♯/F♯ D♯m C♯ B B/A♯ C♯*

1. I'd like to say,_____ that I was on your mind.
2. And Am - ster - dam,_____ I nev - er knew you so well.

Gtr. 2 w/Fig. 1

cont. ad lib.

F♯ C♯/F♯ D♯m C♯ B B/A♯ C♯*

So I phone you at ten past three, in the af - ter - noon._____
The sta - di - um rings_____ with laugh - ter, at ev' - ry turn._____

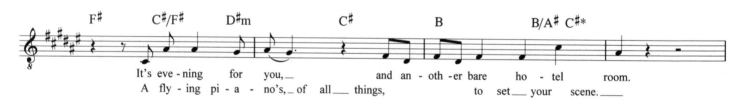

F♯ C♯/F♯ D♯m C♯ B B/A♯ C♯*

It's eve - ning for you,_ and an - oth - er bare ho - tel room.
A fly - ing pi - a - no's,_ of all _ things, to set _ your scene._____

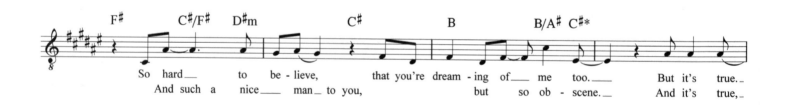

F♯ C♯/F♯ D♯m C♯ B B/A♯ C♯*

So hard_ to be - lieve, that you're dream - ing of _ me too._ But it's true._
And such a nice_ man_ to you, but so ob - scene._ And it's true,_

B C♯

_ girl._ You on - ly go a -

Gtr. 1

f w/dist.

58

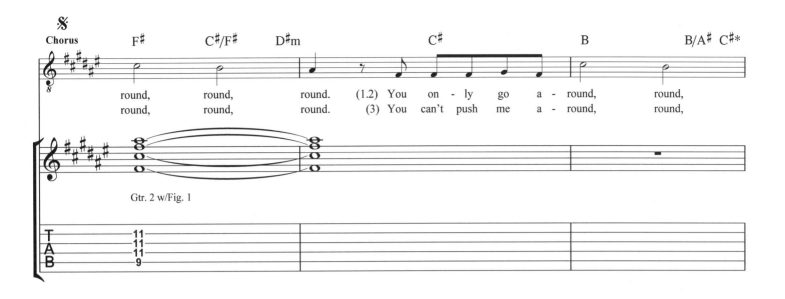

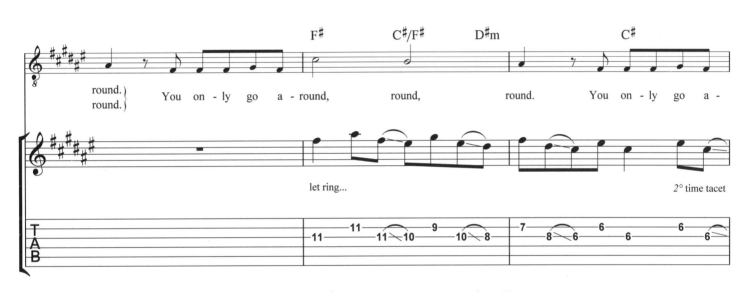

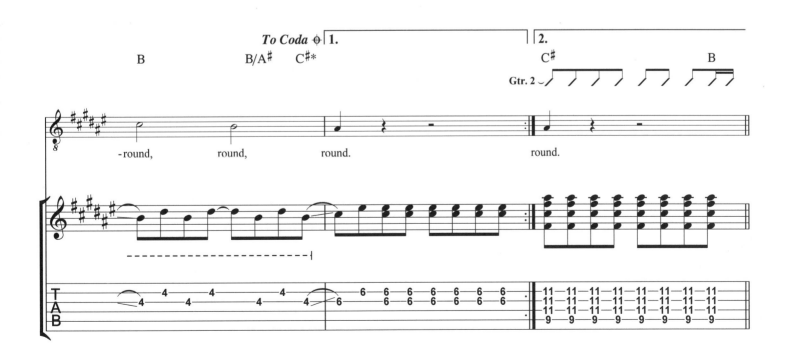

59

Time Awaits

Words & Music by
Luke Pritchard, Hugh Harris, Max Rafferty & Paul Garred

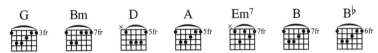

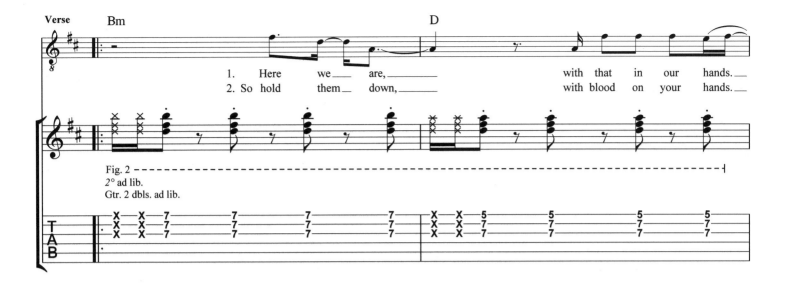

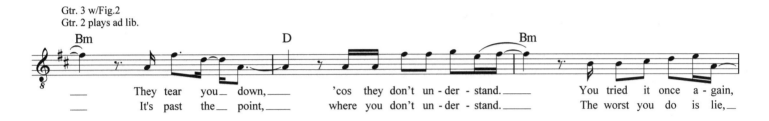

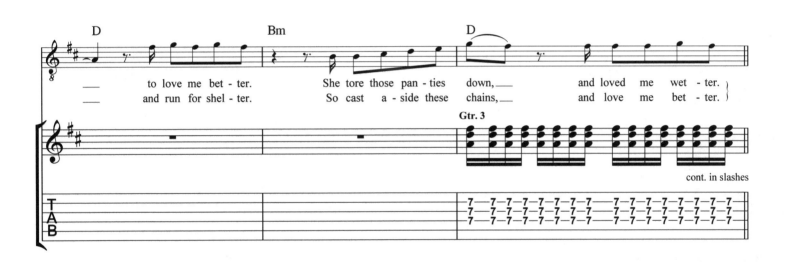

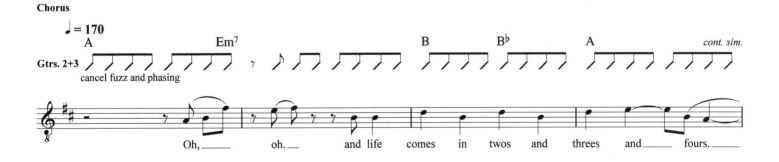

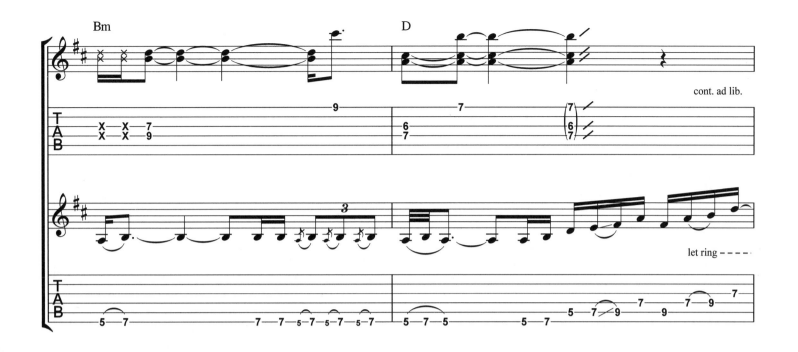

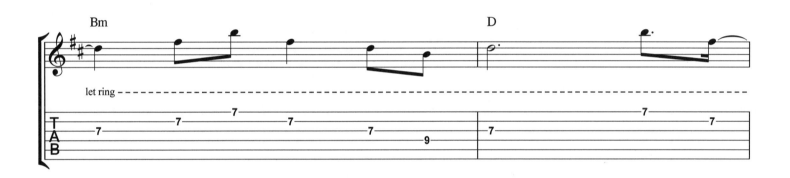

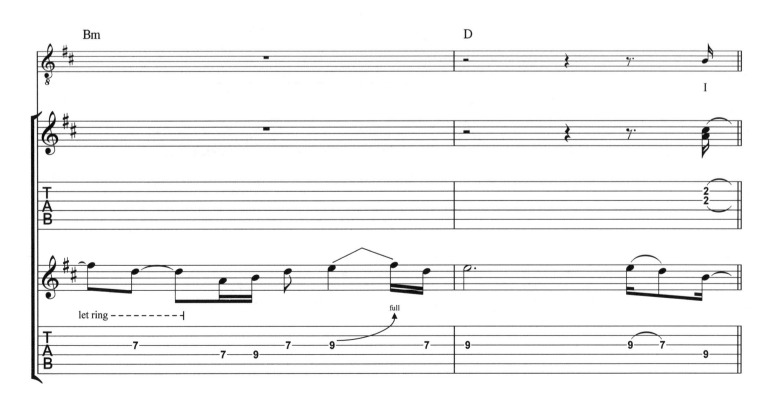

Got No Love

Words & Music by
Luke Pritchard, Hugh Harris, Max Rafferty & Paul Garred

123456789

Guitar Tablature Explained

Guitar music can be notated in three different ways: on a musical stave, in tablature, and in rhythm slashes

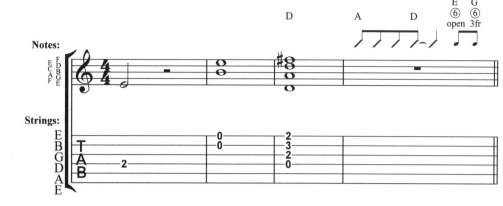

RHYTHM SLASHES: are written above the stave. Strum chords in the rhythm indicated. Round noteheads indicate single notes.

THE MUSICAL STAVE: shows pitches and rhythms and is divided by lines into bars. Pitches are named after the first seven letters of the alphabet.

TABLATURE: graphically represents the guitar fingerboard. Each horizontal line represents a string, and each number represents a fret.

Definitions for special guitar notation

SEMI-TONE BEND: Strike the note and bend up a semi-tone (½ step).

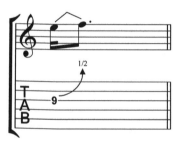

WHOLE-TONE BEND: Strike the note and bend up a whole-tone (full step).

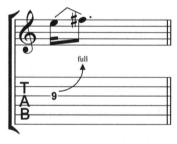

GRACE NOTE BEND: Strike the note and bend as indicated. Play the first note as quickly as possible.

QUARTER-TONE BEND: Strike the note and bend up a ¼ step

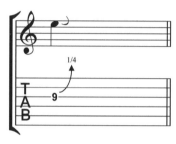

BEND & RELEASE: Strike the note and bend up as indicated, then release back to the original note.

COMPOUND BEND & RELEASE: Strike the note and bend up and down in the rhythm indicated.

PRE-BEND: Bend the note as indicated, then strike it.

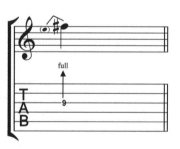

PRE-BEND & RELEASE: Bend the note as indicated. Strike it and release the note back to the original pitch.

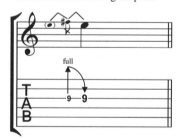

HAMMER-ON: Strike the first note with one finger, then sound the second note (on the same string) with another finger by fretting it without picking.

PULL-OFF: Place both fingers on the note to be sounded, strike the first note and without picking, pull the finger off to sound the second note.

LEGATO SLIDE (GLISS): Strike the first note and then slide the same fret-hand finger up or down to the second note. The second note is not struck.

MUFFLED STRINGS: A percussive sound is produced by laying the first hand across the string(s) without depressing, and striking them with the pick hand.

NATURAL HARMONIC: Strike the note while the fret-hand lightly touches the string directly over the fret indicated.

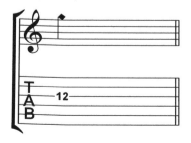

PICK SCRAPE: The edge of the pick is rubbed down (or up) the string, producing a scratchy sound.

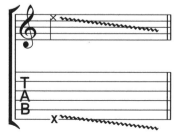

PALM MUTING: The note is partially muted by the pick hand lightly touching the string(s) just before the bridge.

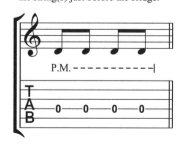

SHIFT SLIDE (GLISS & RESTRIKE) Same as legato slide, except the second note is struck.

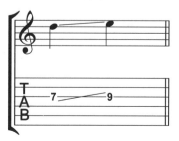

71